ALL AROUND THE WORLD
ARGENTINA

by Kristine Spanier

pogo

Ideas for Parents and Teachers

Pogo Books let children practice reading informational text while introducing them to nonfiction features such as headings, labels, sidebars, maps, and diagrams, as well as a table of contents, glossary, and index.

Carefully leveled text with a strong photo match offers early fluent readers the support they need to succeed.

Before Reading

- "Walk" through the book and point out the various nonfiction features. Ask the student what purpose each feature serves.
- Look at the glossary together. Read and discuss the words.

Read the Book

- Have the child read the book independently.
- Invite him or her to list questions that arise from reading.

After Reading

- Discuss the child's questions. Talk about how he or she might find answers to those questions.
- Prompt the child to think more. Ask: Have you seen a cowboy or gaucho before? Would you like to?

Pogo Books are published by Jump!
5357 Penn Avenue South
Minneapolis, MN 55419
www.jumplibrary.com

Library of Congress Cataloging-in-Publication Data

Names: Spanier, Kristine, author.
Title: Argentina : all around the world / by Kristine Spanier.
Description: Minneapolis, MN : Jump!, Inc., 2020.
Series: All around the world | "Pogo Books."
Includes bibliographical references and index.
Identifiers: LCCN 2018040683 (print)
LCCN 2018042596 (ebook)
ISBN 9781641286404 (ebook)
ISBN 9781641286381 (hardcover : alk. paper)
ISBN 9781641286398 (pbk.)
Subjects: LCSH: Argentina—Juvenile literature.
Classification: LCC F2808.2 (ebook)
LCC F2808.2 .S65 2019 (print) | DDC 982—dc23
LC record available at https://lccn.loc.gov/2018040683

Editor: Susanne Bushman
Designer: Molly Ballanger

Photo Credits: saiko3p/Shutterstock, cover; BODY Philippe/Hemis/SuperStock, 1; Pixfiction/Shutterstock, 3; Det-anan/Shutterstock, 4; Diego Grandi/Shutterstock, 5; naphtalina/iStock, 6-7; pawopa3336/iStock, 8t; Filip Faxa/Shutterstock, 8b; kavram/iStock, 8-9t; Oleg Senkov/Shutterstock, 8-9b; ANDREYGUDKOV/iStock, 10-11; sunsinger/Shutterstock, 12; Jeff Greenberg/age fotostock/SuperStock, 13; A. Parada/Alamy, 14-15; bonchan/Shutterstock, 16; Aleksandr_Vorobev/iStock, 17; Javier Etcheverry/VW PICS/UIG/Getty Images, 18-19; Nick Albi/Shutterstock, 20-21; dario hayashi/Shutterstock, 23.

Printed in the United States of America at Corporate Graphics in North Mankato, Minnesota.

TABLE OF CONTENTS

CHAPTER 1

WELCOME TO ARGENTINA!

Iguazú Falls

Gaze at the powerful Iguazú Falls. See icy **glaciers**. Dance the **tango**. Welcome to Argentina!

The widest street in the world is in Buenos Aires. An **obelisk** stands in the middle of the Avenue of July 9. It stands for pride. July 9, 1816, is when the country gained **independence**. From what country? Spain.

obelisk

Buenos Aires is the **capital**. The **president** has an office here. It is called the Casa Rosada. It means the pink house!

WHAT DO YOU THINK?

In this country, the law states that everyone 18 and older must vote. Do you think voting should be required? Why or why not?

Casa Rosada

Aconcagua

Patagonia

Pampas

Tierra del Fuego

The Andes Mountains are in the west. Aconcagua is South America's tallest peak. It is 22,831 feet (6,959 meters) high. In the center are **plains** called the Pampas. Patagonia is in the far south. It is cold enough for glaciers here!

Tierra del Fuego is an area of islands. It is at the southern tip of South America. It is divided between Argentina and Chile.

What animals are here? You will find guanacos and alpacas in the northwest. Llamas, too. Parrots and canaries fly the skies in the south.

DID YOU KNOW?

Many **crops** grow here. Like what? Wheat. Corn. Sunflowers. The seeds are used to make cooking oil.

guanaco ·····▶

CHAPTER 2

LIFE IN ARGENTINA

Some parts of Argentina are **rural**. People in small towns use horses to travel. Or they ride in horse-drawn carts.

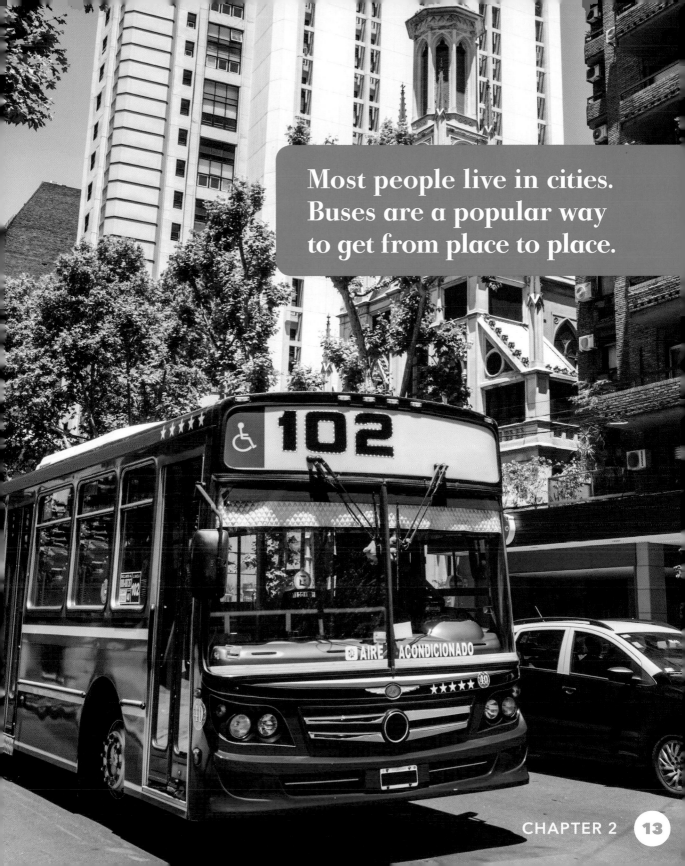

Most people live in cities. Buses are a popular way to get from place to place.

Children go to school when they are six years old. Half go during the first part of the day. The other half goes in the afternoon. Students learn English. Most students wear uniforms over regular clothes. They look like lab coats.

WHAT DO YOU THINK?

Students decide if they will go to high school to prepare for college. Or they may go to a **trade school** to train for a job instead. What path would you choose? Why?

uniform ·····▶

CHAPTER 3

FOOD AND FUN

What do people eat here?
Empanadas are turnovers
filled with meat and vegetables.
Asado is also popular.
It is barbecued meat.

empanada

People drink a tea called mate. When a group drinks from the same straw it is a sign of friendship.

straw

mate

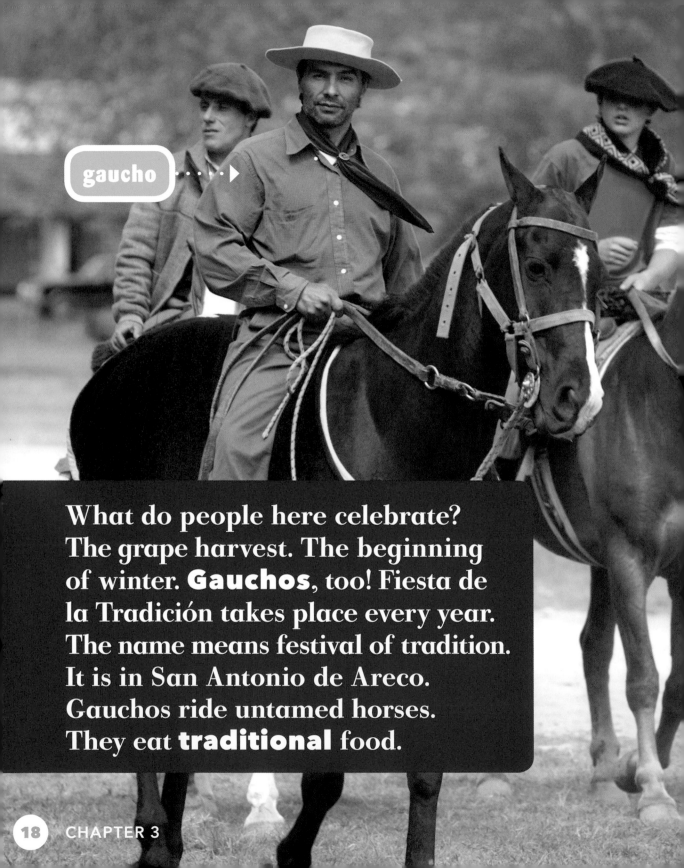

gaucho · · · · ▸

What do people here celebrate? The grape harvest. The beginning of winter. **Gauchos**, too! Fiesta de la Tradición takes place every year. The name means festival of tradition. It is in San Antonio de Areco. Gauchos ride untamed horses. They eat **traditional** food.

TAKE A LOOK!

Gauchos wear traditional outfits at the festival. They have many pieces to them. Horses have special saddles, too.

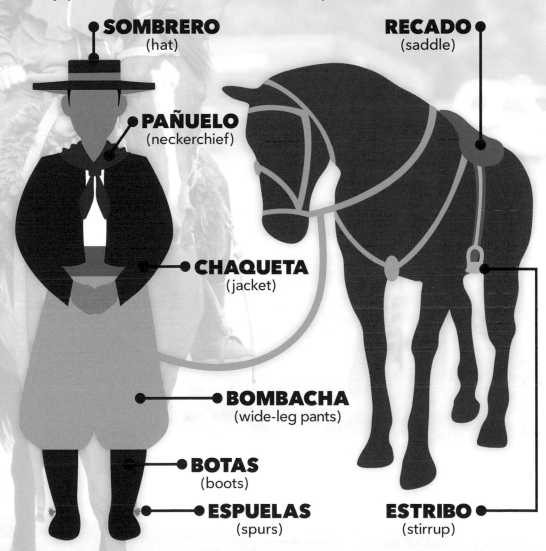

SOMBRERO
(hat)

RECADO
(saddle)

PAÑUELO
(neckerchief)

CHAQUETA
(jacket)

BOMBACHA
(wide-leg pants)

BOTAS
(boots)

ESPUELAS
(spurs)

ESTRIBO
(stirrup)

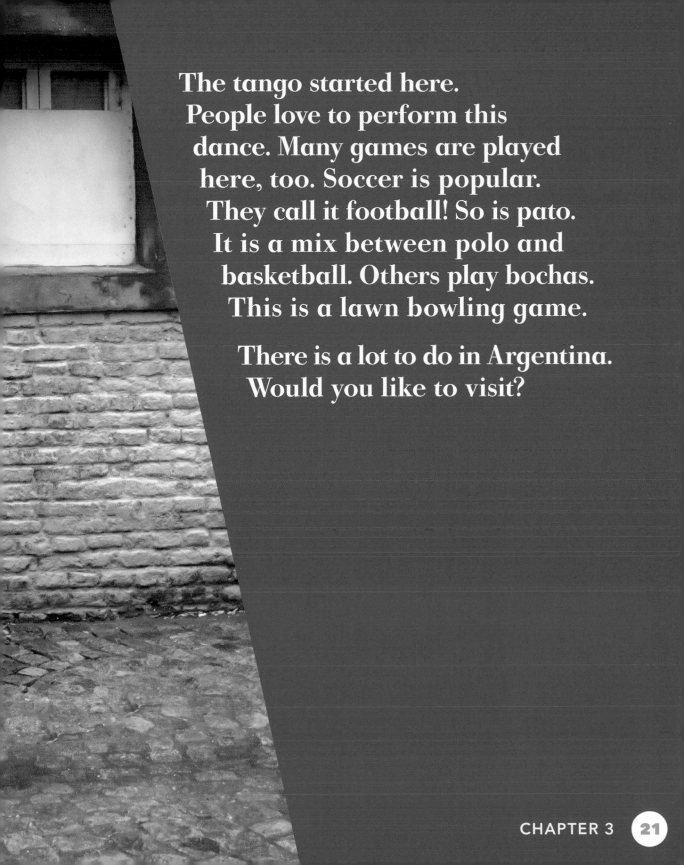

The tango started here. People love to perform this dance. Many games are played here, too. Soccer is popular. They call it football! So is pato. It is a mix between polo and basketball. Others play bochas. This is a lawn bowling game.

There is a lot to do in Argentina. Would you like to visit?

QUICK FACTS & TOOLS

ARGENTINA

Location: southern South America

Size: 1,073,518 square miles
(2,780,400 square kilometers)

Population: 44,694,198
(July 2018 estimate)

Capital: Buenos Aires

Type of Government:
presidential republic

Language: Spanish

Exports: soybeans, petroleum,
gas, vehicles, corn, wheat

Currency: Argentine peso

capital: A city where government leaders meet.

crops: Plants grown for food.

gauchos: Cowboys of the South American Pampas.

glaciers: Very large, slow-moving masses of ice.

independence: Freedom from a controlling authority.

obelisk: A four-sided pillar that becomes narrower toward the top and ends in a pyramid.

plains: Large, flat areas of land.

president: The leader of a country.

rural: Related to the country and country life.

tango: A ballroom dance marked by pauses between steps and a variety of body postures.

trade school: A school to learn a particular trade or craft, especially one that requires working with the hands or with machines.

traditional: Having to do with the customs, beliefs, or activities that are handed down from one generation to the next.

Argentina's currency

INDEX

TO LEARN MORE

Finding more information is as easy as 1, 2, 3.

1. Go to www.factsurfer.com
2. Enter "Argentina" into the search box.
3. Click the "Surf" button to see a list of websites.

FACT SURFER